T0059423

# Where Is Chichen Itza?

by Paula K. Manzanero

illustrated by Dede Putra

Penguin Workshop

For Debbie Guy-Christiansen,
my friend and fellow traveler—PM

PENGUIN WORKSHOP
An Imprint of Penguin Random House LLC, New York

Copyright © 2020 by Penguin Random House LLC. All rights reserved.
Published by Penguin Workshop, an imprint of Penguin Random House LLC, New York.
PENGUIN and PENGUIN WORKSHOP are trademarks of Penguin Books Ltd.
WHO HQ & Design is a registered trademark of Penguin Random House LLC.
Printed in the USA.

Visit us online at www.penguinrandomhouse.com.

Library of Congress Cataloging-in-Publication Data is available upon request.

ISBN 9780593093443 (paperback)          10 9 8 7 6 5 4 3 2 1
ISBN 9780593093450 (library binding)     10 9 8 7 6 5 4 3 2 1

# Contents

John Lloyd Stephens and
Frederick Catherwood

# Where Is Chichen Itza?

In 1839, two men—Frederick Catherwood and John Lloyd Stephens—were on their way to Central America. The US president was sending them there to seal a trade agreement. But the men were also adventurers. Between them, they had already explored Egypt, Greece, and the ancient site of Petra in Jordan. They decided that once their work for the US government was finished, they would look for "ruined cities, places, scenes, and monuments."

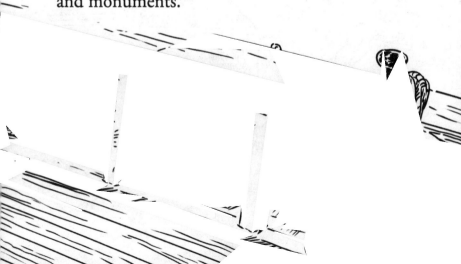

Leaving from New York, they sailed to the Gulf of Honduras. From there, they traveled up the Rio Dulce (Sweet River) to Guatemala City. Then, from the heart of Guatemala, Catherwood and Stephens began to explore the jungles of Central America.

For more than a year, the two men traveled with mules and teams of local guides. They went south to Honduras and then back up through El Salvador, Guatemala, and Mexico. They found ancient ruins, mysterious temples, and stone carvings.

In 1841, they made another trip to explore the northern part of the Yucatan Peninsula. This is the land that separates the Gulf of Mexico and the Caribbean Sea. This time, they traveled with their guides by horseback. They battled mosquitoes and the malaria the insects carried with them. They moved tangled jungle vines to reveal temples and palaces that had not been seen in hundreds of years. From the Mexican town of Merida they traveled to Mayapan and found small—but impressive—ancient sites all along the way.

They had been exploring Central America for a total of about three years when they came upon a most amazing sight—a huge stepped pyramid and massive ball court. They had seen fine examples of the architecture of the Maya— the native people of parts of Mexico and Central America—all along their journey. But here they saw an astonishing arrangement of columns,

a tower with a spiral staircase, and hundreds of carved inscriptions. They were thrilled to find the remains of a city—Chichen Itza.

In time, it became clear that Chichen Itza had been one of the most important and powerful cities of the ancient Maya civilization.

Stephens and Catherwood's discovery proved that the Americas had not been populated by primitive cultures. The ancient Maya people had developed mathematical systems, writing, amazing architecture, beautiful artwork, and the ability to chart the stars and planets in the sky.

The two explorers not only discovered the ruins of the Maya, they made a record of them (in Frederick Catherwood's detailed drawings and John Stephens's journals). They opened a world for people who knew next to nothing of the history of Native Americans, the culture of the Maya, and their truly magnificent accomplishments.

# CHAPTER 1
## World of the Maya

By around the year 500, the Maya civilization in Mesoamerica was reaching its peak. The most important royal families had established powerful cities throughout Central America from present-day Honduras in the south to Mexico's Yucatan Peninsula in the north. For over seven hundred years—from around AD 250 to 900—there was intense building, and constant battling between Maya power centers. During that time, the region they covered was around 120,000 square miles, nearly the same size as the state of New Mexico. The population may have reached up to fifteen million people!

Although there were between forty and fifty notable city-states, there was no single king of the entire region. Each city had its own king or queen who governed over the people in their area and performed important rituals for them.

# Timeline of the Maya

The history of the Maya is divided into three major time periods. Their story begins with the Preclassic Period, which lasted from about 1800 BC to AD 250. This is when small kingdoms, called city-states, were established. Next came the Classic Period, when the Maya greatly expanded and accomplished so many of their most amazing achievements. The final time period, the Postclassic, lasted from 900 to 1524 and marked the beginning of the end of the ancient Maya.

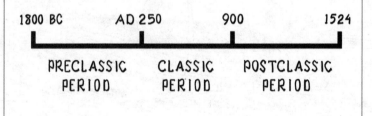

The Maya called their mountain regions the highlands and the areas closer to sea level the lowlands. Even deep in the jungles, they established trade routes with other city-states along inland rivers, coastal waters, and paved pathways.

The Maya worshipped many gods. In each city, the biggest temple was devoted to one of the major gods.

## Who's Who Among the Gods

There are at least two hundred different gods represented in the religious world of the Maya. Although all the city-states shared the same gods, many of them were given more than one name. The Maya felt that the gods controlled their lives and the entire universe. Some of their most important gods were:

Bahlam: jaguar god of the underworld

Camazotz: bat god

Chaac: god of storms and rain

Hunhau: god of death and the underworld

Bahlam

**Itzamná, Itzamana, or sometimes just Zamn:**

**creator god (and perhaps the most important god)**

Itzamná

**Ix Chel: goddess of medicine and childbirth**

**Kinich Ahau: sun god**

**Kukulkan: vision god, represented by a feathered serpent**

**Sip: god of hunting**

Much of the landscape of the Maya is covered with tropical rain forest. It is home to animals such as toucans, tapirs, jaguars, bats, macaws, and

Tapir

snakes. These animals were revered by the ancient Maya and were often represented in their art and religious ceremonies. However, they fished and hunted more common birds and animals like deer for food.

Macaw

The Maya were skilled farmers who cleared parts of the rain forest to grow their crops. Their farms produced corn, beans, chili peppers, and squash. They gathered honey, cotton, and cacao (say: cuh-COW) pods from the trees of the rain forest. They harvested the cacao seeds from the pods to make a foamy drink that tasted like bitter chocolate.

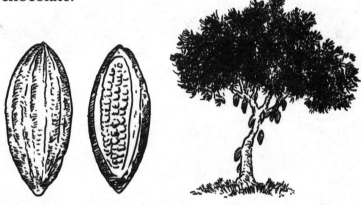

Cacao pods and tree

Corn—which they called *maize*—was their most important crop. They roasted it, ground it, and even crushed it to make drinks and thicken stews.

The Maya paid close attention to their appearance. Both Maya men and women wore their hair long. They decorated their bodies with paint, and sometimes elaborate tattoos and piercings. They wore thin cotton coverings, similar to ponchos, over their shoulders, and

sandals on their feet. The women wore skirts
underneath their long tops. They used embroidery
to decorate their clothing. The designs of their
tattoos, embroidery, and body paint were always
carefully chosen symbols that were important to
each person.

# Maya or Mayan?

The ancient city of Mayapan, near the town of Merida on Mexico's Yucatan Peninsula, was one of the last important city-states for the Maya. It had been long abandoned by the time the Spanish arrived in the 1500s. But they used the

word *Maya* to describe the language of the native people of the Yucatan. By the early 1800s, the word was mistakenly used to describe the people as well as their language.

Today, the word *Mayan* is used only to refer to the language of the Maya people.

Only a few people in this ancient culture could read and write. Some kings and priests (called shamans) were educated. However, it was mainly the scribes who created a written record of Maya life. They recorded stories about the religion, politics, and history of their people. They made records of royal families and important events, like marriages, battles, and major wars.

Using around eight hundred different symbols, called glyphs, scribes wrote books on folded tree bark. Their glyphs represented people, words, sounds, and numbers. This writing system was the most advanced of all ancient Native American cultures. Although only a handful of these books have survived, Maya scribes also helped craftsmen carve thousands of glyphs onto buildings and stone pillars, called stelae. These stelae serve as historical records of the world of the Maya that are still studied today.

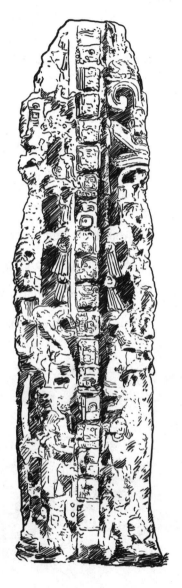

Stela from
Copan, Honduras

## Cracking the Code

The glyphs the Maya used to tell stories about their kings, queens, gods, and major historical events meant nothing to the outside world until well into the twentieth century. In the 1980s, an American teenager named David Stuart finally cracked the code of the Mayan glyphs! He had traveled to Mexico and Guatemala many times with his father, an archaeologist.

David Stuart

It occurred to David that glyphs didn't always represent one word, but sometimes represented sounds, and could express more than one idea. His ideas helped scholars read and understand the glyphs that they had struggled with for decades.

Today, David Stuart is a professor and an archaeologist who continues to study Maya art, images, and glyphs.

The ancient Maya were skilled city planners, architects, and builders. They designed many great palaces, temples, and monuments out of stone. The Maya believed that their universe was divided into three parts: earth, sky, and underworld. They built their pyramids to resemble mountains, reaching high up to the sky. These impressive structures often stood at the ceremonial centers of Maya life and culture.

The community would gather in plazas surrounding the pyramids at special times of year for religious events and to celebrate important occasions for their city-state. For the Maya, each spectacular building and monument was a symbol of the power of their ruling family and also a reminder of their connection to the universe.

# CHAPTER 2
## People on the Move

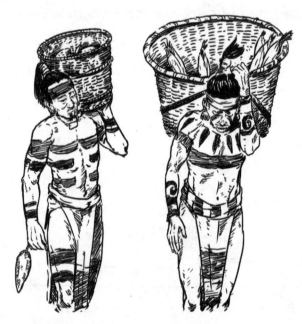

Beginning around AD 800, long droughts (low rainfall) and increased warfare had weakened southern city-states. Without enough rain, farmers could not grow enough food to feed armies on the march and large city populations.

Even though they cut down more and more of the rain forest to plant crops, the people were starving. They wondered if the gods were punishing them. And they may have begun to question the authority of their kings.

Many Maya migrated north, some to Chichen Itza, which became a huge fifteen-square-mile city. Even during the droughts, the city had access to underground water and reservoirs. It became the home of citizens from many other previously independent states. That's why the carvings,

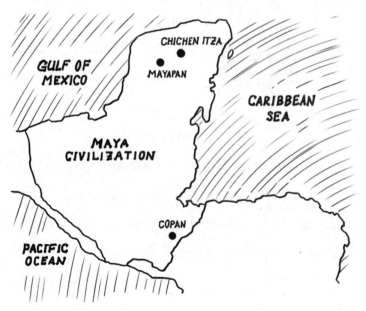

glyphs, and buildings at Chichen Itza represent a combination of styles. Some were elaborately detailed, and others were simple and quite plain.

Unlike other ancient Maya cities, Chichen Itza had no king. The people in government may have been elected by noble families and the high priests of Kukulkan (say: koo-kool-CAN), the feathered snake god that the city was built to honor. Kukulkan was thought of as the Vision Serpent, the messenger who traveled between the Maya kings and their gods.

Kukulkan

The wealthy and important families of Chichen Itza lived in stone homes that were painted with colorful murals. They were big enough to host large parties. Not far from the huge central pyramid, a market filled with an amazing variety of items served the noble families' every need. Fruit and vegetables, salt, cotton, feathers, tools, precious stones, and copper were sold there. The city's connections to other communities made it a trading center like no other in this area.

The more common people of Chichen Itza, the farmers and laborers, were not so fancy. They lived in wooden houses with thatched roofs woven from palm leaves and tall grasses. They grew their own corn, chili peppers, and other vegetables. They hunted in the surrounding forests.

The most powerful families organized spectacular events and displays dedicated to Kukulkan. These festivals were for all the citizens of the city. Everyone took part in ceremonies, rituals, and games in and around the great courtyard of Chichen Itza. It was big enough to hold many thousands of people.

The festivals in honor of Kukulkan drew religious travelers as well. The spread of the worship of the feathered serpent god—as far away as Guatemala—shows the city's growing might throughout the world of the Maya.

# CHAPTER 3
## At the Edge of the Well of Itza

The city of Chichen Itza was built up from the existing settlement around the year 600. By 900, it had grown to become one of the most powerful economic, religious, political, and scientific centers in the Americas. At its height, more than 50,000 people lived there. With its paved roads, the city grew rich selling and trading salt, furs, feathers, cacao, and valuable stones like obsidian.

# Obsidian

Obsidian is a type of glass formed from cooled volcanic lava. It can be sharpened into a very thin blade. It was often used by ancient cultures to make arrowheads and knives. The obsidian was carved into flat blades that were then mounted in a wooden handle. This bladed club was called a macuahuitl (say: MA-ca-WE-til)—very sharp and very dangerous!

Most of the obsidian found at Maya sites is from present-day Guatemala, where some volcanoes are still active today.

The name *Chichen Itza* means "at the edge of the well of Itza." The word *Itza* refers to the Itza Maya people, who controlled the northern region of the Yucatan, known as the Itza State.

The "well" of Itza may refer to the Sacred Cenote at Chichen Itza. It is two hundred feet wide and almost perfectly round. It is enclosed by walls that drop more than sixty feet straight down to the water below.

Sacred Cenote at Chichen Itza

A cenote (say: sen-OH-tay) is a sinkhole or pit formed in limestone rock that exposes underground water. They are clear pools of filtered rainwater that often connect to large underground cave systems. Cenotes can be found at sea level near coastal areas. In Mexico's Yucatan Peninsula, there are thought to be more than six thousand of them.

Cenote in the Yucatan Peninsula

To the ancient Maya, cenotes were a source of fresh drinking water, sacred sites for worship, and a link to the underworld (their concept of life after death).

Because the limestone cave systems supplied fresh water to the people in the Yucatan, they were sacred to the Maya. The caves were used to channel water for irrigating crops. Sacrificial offerings to the gods were also placed inside them.

The cenote cave systems and wide paved roads connected the center of Chichen Itza to surrounding communities.

Some archaeologists who have studied the plan of Chichen Itza see a reflection of our solar system in its layout.

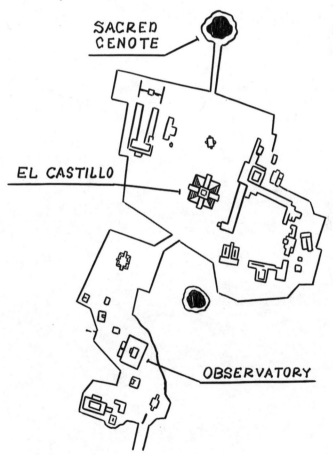

SACRED CENOTE

EL CASTILLO

OBSERVATORY

At its northern point is the holy site: the Sacred Cenote. The southern point is marked by an observatory that may represent the planet Earth. And at its center sits the mighty pyramid called El Castillo. El Castillo represents the sun. The pyramid was also the center of life in the ancient city of Chichen Itza.

# CHAPTER 4
## El Castillo

El Castillo is not the tallest pyramid ever built by the ancient Maya. Still, its base covers a huge area. Each side of the pyramid is 181 feet wide. It stands 79 feet tall, with a temple building at the top. The total height of the structure is 98 feet.

The Maya were among the first civilizations to understand the number zero and create a symbol to represent it. This allowed them to make very accurate measurements.

Their advanced number system helped the Maya to build amazingly engineered structures. The pyramid at Chichen Itza is no exception. The entire building functions as a kind of calendar. Each of the four sides of the pyramid has 91 steps. There is an additional step at the very top of the platform. So the total number of steps is 365—the number of days in a year. At the base of one of the staircases are two massive openmouthed snake heads carved from stone.

# Maya Math

The Maya based their number system on groups of twenty. The glyphs for each number were drawn using only three simple symbols: a shell represented zero, a pebble stood for one, and a stick equaled five. These are the glyphs for the numbers zero through nineteen, the first twenty numbers of the Maya counting system:

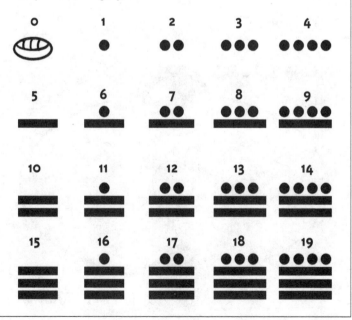

The carved snake heads represent Kukulkan's face. There is no stone body of the god. Instead, his "body" is seen in the shadows along the staircase. This happens only twice a year, around March 21 and September 23, on the spring and fall equinoxes. (The day when the sun crosses the earth's equator, and is closest to it, is called an equinox.) On these days, Earth's northern and southern hemispheres get an equal amount of sunlight. Day and night are the same length: twelve hours each.

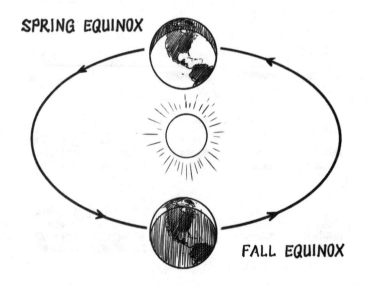

SPRING EQUINOX

FALL EQUINOX

In the late afternoon on those two days, the serpent shadow appears to slither down the pyramid. It represents Kukulkan's return to earth, and was probably understood as a blessing on the Maya people. Because the ruling families of Chichen Itza could predict the seemingly magical appearance of this god so precisely, it probably made them seem even more powerful.

# The Sounds of Chichen Itza

If you stand in the field at the base of El Castillo and clap, an echo will come back—not as a clap, but as the chirp of a bird! A clap from the edge of the massive ball court will produce exactly nine clap echoes back. And standing high on the temple on the north side of the court, it is possible to hear a whisper from 150 feet away!

At other Maya ruins, small temple rooms at the very tops of pyramids can actually amplify voices and may have acted as ancient megaphones. Some Maya experts believe that kings and priests used sound tricks like these to astonish and impress their people.

The entire pyramid is built from a type of rock called limestone. The builders didn't have to go far to find it. The whole Yucatan Peninsula is a flat limestone plain. The Maya miners worked in quarries and cut the rock less than a third of a mile away from the building site.

The pyramid was built between the years 800 and 900. But El Castillo wasn't built all at once. It was actually constructed over an earlier pyramid that was, in fact, built over yet an even earlier structure. This was not uncommon for the Maya, who often built new pyramids on top of older ones. Using this method, new rulers could constantly enlarge buildings, impress the people, and create bigger monuments to their gods and themselves.

Both El Castillo and the earlier pyramid inside it have nine levels. But the older structure has only one set of steps. Inside a chamber in the older pyramid is a throne shaped like a jaguar. It is painted red and has green jade for its eyes. The Maya often used images of jaguars to represent powerful kings or fierce warriors. They admired jaguars for their strength, speed, and hunting skills. And, unlike most cats, jaguars aren't afraid to enter water. They are strong swimmers. For

Jaguar-shaped throne
in El Castillo

this reason, and for the belief that the jaguar could see in the dark, the jaguar was also a Maya symbol of the underworld, the place where water "lived" underground.

El Castillo was built in the center of four cenotes. They are directly to the north, south, east, and west of the huge pyramid. The largest is the Sacred Cenote to the north.

For the Maya, the underworld was a series of underground rivers and caves. Cenotes were the entrance to this land of the dead—a place of great fear, thought to be ruled by the gods of death.

A cave from the Maya underworld

The Maya offered sacrifices to these gods by submerging valuable objects into cenotes. Some of the objects that have been removed from the Sacred Cenote include pottery, jade, obsidian, and gold.

There is another cenote—a fifth one—that sits directly under the pyramid and holds enough water to fill six Olympic swimming pools! This giant cenote indicates that El Castillo's location was very important. It links the caves of the underworld to the earth (the pyramid itself) and the sky—the temple high atop El Castillo.

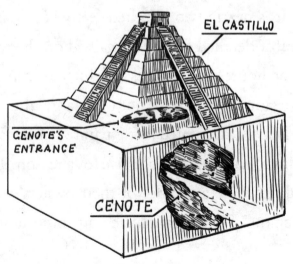

# CHAPTER 5
## Life in the Big City

Although it's clear that El Castillo was the most important structure at Chichen Itza, one of the biggest buildings is called Las Monjas (say: loss MOHN-hoss). It is believed to have been a palace for Maya noble families, one that was rebuilt and enlarged many times. It contains more rooms than any other building at Chichen Itza. It is nearly two hundred feet wide. Some of the most detailed glyphs are carved on the walls.

The houses and palaces of Chichen Itza's most important families were not only large, they were also heavily decorated with painted murals and carvings. They were impressive for a reason. These buildings were a symbol of their owners' wealth and status. The rulers of such an important city

Las Monjas

had a big responsibility to the people who lived and worked there. It was their duty to run the city. But they also organized a popular game that served as a kind of ritual to promote their city.

The Maya ball game called Pok-a-Tok was both a game and a sacred religious event. Two teams of up to seven players tried to get a rubber ball through a stone ring, or hoop, attached to a wall. They couldn't use their hands or feet to score— only their hips, knees, and elbows.

The largest such ball court in the world is located in Chichen Itza. Its two parallel walls are 312 feet long, and the field itself is 545 feet long.

The stone rings on each wall are four feet across and carved with snake designs. They are about twenty feet off the ground! The Maya used natural latex (a sticky, milky liquid) from rubber trees to create solid balls that were bouncy but heavy. To protect themselves, players wore padded belts and head coverings to cushion any hard blows.

Ball court in Chichen Itza

To the Maya, this difficult game may have represented the struggle between life and death. There are stone benches at the ball court at Chichen Itza. A carving on one of them shows a headless ballplayer. It is thought that the losing captain—or maybe even the entire losing team—may have been sacrificed as a gift to their gods! The game might have been played to settle disputes between cities. The players were trained to be both athletes and warriors. Some historians believe that the winning team may have been "honored" to die instead.

But why was human sacrifice so important to the Maya? They believed their gods needed to be fed so that the Maya civilization could remain strong. Human life was the ultimate gift to honor their gods. High-ranking people, like warriors, prisoners of war, or Pok-a-Tok athletes were most often killed as sacrifices.

It was common for the Maya to remove the heart of the person they were sacrificing, using a very sharp obsidian knife. This would most often have been done at the top of a pyramid temple,

in a show for the people gathered below. Bodies were sometimes thrown down the pyramid stairway, where the heads might be removed. These were collected and exhibited for the community.

The Maya displayed the heads of prisoners, enemies, and sacrificed ballplayers in rows,

impaled on wooden posts. These skull racks—
or skull walls—showed off the conquests of
a particular state or city. At Chichen Itza, the
Platform of the Skulls is carved to re-create the
look of a skull rack. The platform is covered in
images of more than five hundred skulls, eagles,
snakes, and warriors carrying human heads.

People were also thrown into the Sacred Cenote at Chichen Itza as human sacrifices. The straight sides of this cenote and the deep water made it impossible to climb out or escape. It's believed that sacrifices into the Sacred Cenote were not warriors or prisoners. They were people who were offered up to the gods in times of drought. The hope was that the gods would send more rain to fill the cenotes with fresh water again, make their crops grow, and keep Maya civilization stable.

# CHAPTER 6
## Temple of the Warriors

In Chichen Itza, the Temple of the Warriors was built to honor Chaac, the god of rain. Chaac is often pictured carrying an ax that he uses to strike the clouds in order to make rain and thunder. The Temple  of the Warriors looks like a flattened pyramid. The four levels were built on top of a smaller pyramid, which was called the Temple of the Chacmool.

Chacmools (or Chac-Mools) are statues of

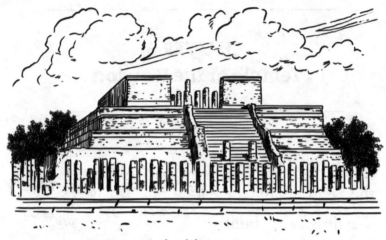

Temple of the Warriors

young men, half sitting up, resting on their elbows with their knees drawn in. Their stomachs are flat and may have been used to hold a bowl or plate for offerings. We can't be sure if they were messengers from the god Chaac, or used to carry offerings to him. There is a Chacmool at Chichen Itza who wears ear ornaments with tiny images of the god Chaac carved into them. Was the plate

Chacmool

he carries used to hold sacrifices to the god of rain?

Some scholars believe that it's not so important what the Chacmools are holding, but what they are looking at. Their heads are always turned either to the right or left. They are never shown looking straight ahead. Often, Chacmools seem to be positioned to "watch" other buildings and maybe even to observe the planets and stars.

These puzzling figures appear not only at Chichen Itza but also from Central Mexico to the Caribbean coast, and were important not just to the Maya but also to the Aztec, another ancient American civilization.

Aztec Chacmool in Mexico City

In the city of Chichen Itza, the Chacmools appear to be dressed as warriors. At the top of the Temple of the Warriors sits a statue of a large Chacmool, staring at El Castillo. Behind it are two pillars carved to look like Kukulkan, the feathered serpent.

Along the southern side of the temple is the Group of a Thousand Columns. This site actually contains about two hundred round and square columns—far fewer than a thousand—that at one time probably held up a roof made of thatched leaves. The square columns are carved with images of warriors.

To the south of these columns lies a small building called the Temple of the Carved Columns, which contains more warrior-carved columns and an altar with yet another Chacmool.

In total, there are fourteen Chacmools at Chichen Itza. Their presence shows how important it was to keep the god of rain happy.

# CHAPTER 7
## Looking to the Sky

The Maya studied the solar system and tracked the movement of the sun, moon, planets, and stars. They did all this without modern instruments like telescopes. They recorded their observations and used them to plan nearly every part of their lives, from farming to waging war. They used their skills as astronomers to create a series of highly accurate calendars. In fact, of all the world's ancient calendar systems, the Maya's was the most complex.

Maya astronomers kept track of the passage of time by observing the motions of the planets. And they faithfully recorded what they saw. Because the Maya believed that the gods guided the sun and moon across the sky, they performed regular rituals and sacrifices to help keep all the planets, as well as the sun and moon, moving along on their journeys.

# The Maya Calendars

The Maya kept track of time by following a continuous cycle of days in three different calendars.

Every number and day of the 260-day Sacred Calendar (also called the Round Count) had its own meaning, based on different gods and directions.

Round Count calendar

The 365-day Haab Calendar was divided into eighteen groups of twenty days each (plus five additional "unlucky" days!). These two calendars together (each shaped like wheels inscribed with many glyphs) could be set in motion to run together. It would take fifty-two years for one calendar cycle to repeat.

The third calendar, called the Long Count, was based on thirteen cycles of four-hundred-year eras called baktuns. The number thirteen was significant to the Maya calendar, and they believed there was a "great cycle" of thirteen baktuns, which lasted 5,125 years. The last cycle actually came to an end on December 21, 2012.

Long Count calendar

The Maya believed that near the end of such a cycle, the old sun ends and a new sun emerges. Using the Long Count, they could calculate dates far into the future and also billions of years into the past!

At Chichen Itza, there is a round building at the top of a large platform, called El Caracol. It was built as an observatory to study the sky. Because the land on the Yucatan is so flat, there is no high jungle growth, so this was easy enough to do. There are sight lines—imaginary marks or threads from the observer to the object—in El Caracol that line up with the position of the sun and many different astronomical events.

El Caracol

The building has a spiral staircase inside its tower. Its doors and windows were designed to see special parts of the sky. Two of the windows each provide a perfect view of the sunset on one of the equinoxes. The spiral of the staircase, along with the entire site of El Caracol itself, seems to have been carefully designed to watch and record the movements of the planet Venus.

To the Maya, there was no planet in the sky more important than Venus. The Maya believed that watching Venus told them the right time to go to war. They also thought that the movements of Venus could predict the future.

Venus in the night sky

Although Venus orbits the sun like the other planets in our solar system, it can appear to simply move back and forth across the sky. This is because from Earth, it appears that Venus goes through four phases: It appears in the night sky after the setting sun; then it disappears for eight days. After that, it appears in the daylight, rising just before dawn, and then disappears, this time for ninety days.

For the Maya, the repetitive cycles of the planet Venus were very significant. Like the game Pok-a-Tok, the return of Venus in the morning may have represented the struggle between life and death. Celebrating the reappearance of this important planet reminded them of their connection to the gods. The Maya calendars and astrology as well as their religion all explained the activities of the gods. The Maya believed their gods constantly replayed their own mythical stories since the time of creation.

For three hundred years, Chichen Itza had been the greatest city of the Maya. But its citizens eventually began to move to much smaller villages and away from the city center. By the year 1200, its population was decreasing, and the noble families of the area had moved on. Why did this happen? No one knows for sure.

A new center of power and trade was established at Mayapan by 1220. Those who remained in and around Chichen Itza used the site only occasionally for the sacred ceremonies that for centuries had been so important. And by 1450, even Mayapan had lost its political power. The Maya had scattered to many small towns.

Although the Maya had developed complex calendars and sophisticated ways of predicting astrological events, they never could have predicted the event that shook their world. It was the arrival of Spanish explorers on the Yucatan Peninsula in 1511, which took the Maya completely by surprise.

# CHAPTER 8
## Invasion of the Spanish

Between the fifteenth and seventeenth centuries, Europeans began to travel across the Atlantic Ocean in search of new trade routes to the Far East and new sources of wealth. Men like Christopher Columbus, Amerigo Vespucci, John Cabot, and Henry Hudson went on voyages of exploration that led to the establishment of colonies in what to them was the New World.

Christopher Columbus

In 1519, the Spanish explorer Hernan Cortes invaded present-day Mexico with about five hundred men. He claimed the land as "New Spain," and within just three years, defeated the Aztec Empire, which had dominated much of present-day central Mexico.

Although the world of the Maya was fading,

there were still many thousands of Maya living throughout the Yucatan. At one point the Spanish decided to make Chichen Itza their capital. Even though the site was already somewhat in ruins and partly overtaken by the jungle, they were impressed by the number of sturdy stone buildings and paved walkways.

# Conquistadors

*Conquistador* (say: kon-KEES-ta-DOR) is the Spanish word for conqueror. These men were noblemen, explorers, and soldiers from Spain and Portugal who sailed from Europe to the Americas beginning in the late fifteenth century. Their goal was to open new trade routes between their countries and other parts of the world. They conquered the lands they thought they had discovered. And for the next three centuries, they fought to control much of this part of the world for Spain and Portugal. They took the land and drove out or killed the people who lived there and, in the process, destroyed their cultures.

Some of the most well-known conquistadors are Juan Ponce de Leon, Francisco Pizarro, Hernando de Soto, and Hernan Cortes.

Juan Ponce de Leon

Francisco Pizarro

The Spanish also found plenty of fresh water from the cenotes. But in 1533, Maya warriors who remained in the area banded together to defeat them. Even though the conquistadors had crossbows, swords, and much more sophisticated weapons, the Maya with their bows and arrows, stones, and obsidian blades drove the Spanish soldiers from the ruins.

The Spanish were not about to give up, however. In 1540, they mounted a serious effort to seize control of the Maya of the Yucatan Peninsula. They thought nothing of the accomplishments of the ancient civilization and the fact that there were still small Maya kingdoms in the region. They burned all but four of the Maya books!

Even so, it took the Spanish much longer to defeat them than they expected. It was not until 1697, nearly 180 years after Cortes had first arrived in Mexico, that the Spanish finally conquered the last Maya city deep in the jungle of what is now part of Guatemala.

After that, the Spaniards built a town near the ruins of Chichen Itza. They used the land as a cattle ranch. They wanted to convert the Maya to their Catholic religion. And so they installed a cannon at the top of El Castillo. There were guards to keep the Maya from returning to the site to worship their gods and perform rituals there. And it was the Spanish who gave the most famous parts of the site the names we still call them today. *El Castillo* means the Castle in Spanish. *El Caracol*—the Spanish word for snail— was the name given to the round observatory with its stone spiral staircase. The building with so many small rooms was *Las Monjas*.

That means the Nuns, or the Nunnery. The Spanish thought it resembled a convent, a place where nuns live.

A hundred and fifty years later, the descendants of the first Spanish soldiers held almost total control over the region. (The land became the country of Mexico.) However, the native Maya people began to revolt against the Mexican army in 1847, in what is called the Caste War of Yucatan. For years, the independent Maya in the southeastern part of the peninsula had skirmishes throughout the northwest. And by 1867, the Maya occupied much of the western part of the Yucatan as well. The war officially ended in 1901, when the Mexican army took over the Maya capital of Chan Santa Cruz, just over a hundred miles south of Chichen Itza.

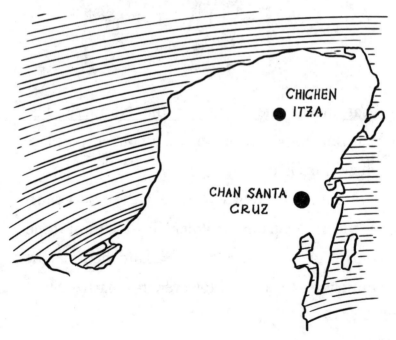

# CHAPTER 9
## Discovering the Past

During their first trip to Central America in 1839–1840, John Stephens and Frederick Catherwood recorded every detail of their long journey. After they returned to New York, Stephens wrote *Incidents of Travel in Yucatan* and Catherwood provided illustrations. The book was published in 1841, and told of their travels  throughout the region. It became a best seller. The world was captivated by tales of unmapped jungles and mysterious stone ruins. American author Edgar Allan Poe said it was "perhaps the most interesting book of travel ever published."

In a time before photography, Catherwood's illustrations were the first images of the region that people had ever seen. Drawn on-site, they were very detailed and exceptionally accurate. *Incidents of Travel in Yucatan* sparked major interest in the art and culture of the ancient Maya.

Then, during their second trip, when they came upon the ruins of Chichen Itza, the pair traveled with an amazing new type of technology that allowed them to depict their astonishing finds. Catherwood had brought a daguerreotype camera with him! (Say: duh-GEH-ruh-tipe.)

When Stephens and Catherwood approached Chichen Itza, they could see the tallest buildings from the road. The land surrounding the ruins was still being used as a large cattle ranch called a hacienda. Because the cows kept the land cleared by grazing on it, the two men could see the details of the ruins very plainly.

# The Daguerreotype

Daguerreotype of Louis Daguerre

Louis Daguerre introduced the first practical photographic process to the public in 1839. It exposed a light-sensitive, polished sheet of silver-plated copper held within a camera. Getting the exposure could take a few seconds or up to a few minutes. The copper plate was then treated with chemicals, rinsed, dried, and sealed under glass to preserve the image. Less than twenty years later, the daguerreotype was replaced by less expensive and quicker methods of photography.

Stephens and Catherwood were impressed by the clear features of what they called "picture writing"—the glyphs of the Maya. They climbed one of the biggest pyramids they had ever seen. And standing at the top, they saw the unique columns of the Temple of the Warriors. Stephens wrote, "I counted three hundred and eighty, and there were many more." At Chichen Itza, the two men explored one of the last great cities to exist before the collapse of the ancient civilization.

In 1842, Stephens and Catherwood left Mexico for New York. After returning home to England in 1843, Catherwood exhibited his latest drawings. In 1844, he published a folio, an oversize book with twenty-five color-tinted illustrations and a map, called *Views of Ancient Monuments in Central America, Chiapas and Yucatan.* As he had earlier, Catherwood captured each glyph and temple carving perfectly. His illustrations from the folio remain surprisingly accurate. Only three hundred copies were printed, and today they are very rare.

Page from Catherwood's 1844 book

Edward Herbert Thompson

It was Stephens's best-selling book that inspired an American named Edward Herbert Thompson to buy the ranch that included the site of Chichen Itza. Once there, he rebuilt the large plantation house on the estate, which had been destroyed during the Caste War of Yucatan. He began dredging the Sacred Cenote in 1904, uncovering objects as well as human skeletons that the Maya had placed there as offerings hundreds of years before.

But in 1926, the government of Mexico challenged Thompson. They felt he had removed these objects from the cenote illegally. They felt the ancient Maya offerings belonged to the Mexican people.

Thompson at the Sacred Cenote

After the Mexican Revolution, ancient ruins became a source of national pride. The Mexican government began protecting ruins and historical sites from looters—thieves who came to steal the remarkable treasures. Scholarly archaeological excavations began in Chichen Itza in the 1930s. That was when the older and smaller pyramid was discovered under the surface of El Castillo.

# The Mexican Revolution

The Mexican Revolution, also known as the Mexican Civil War, began in 1910 with a political revolt. It quickly grew into a war with many different sides. Wealthy, established government forces faced revolutionary leaders as well as loosely organized bands of civilians who waged small but violent attacks.

Because there were many leaders and sides in the war, it was easy for outside governments—including the United States—to influence the fighting. In the end, the revolutionaries won, but it is estimated that as many as 1.5 million Mexican people may have died in the decade-long war. The establishment of the Mexican Constitution in 1917 helped bring about an end to the conflict.

The even smaller and oldest interior structure inside that was not discovered until 2016. The Sacred Cenote was explored and dredged again in the 1950s. And the work at Chichen Itza continued throughout the twentieth century and into the twenty-first.

El Castillo and the Temple of the Warriors

were restored. It was only recently that the cenote under El Castillo was revealed.

In 1972, a Mexican law was passed to protect Chichen Itza and other sites and monuments. The ruins and the entire site are now managed by the National Institute of Anthropology and History, based in Mexico City.

## The Hacienda Chichen

A man named Fernando Barbachano Peon bought the hacienda from Edward Thompson's family in 1944. He turned the cattle ranch's main house into a hotel called the Hacienda Chichen. It sits right next to the ruins of Chichen Itza.

Barbachano realized the value in creating interest in the culture of the Maya and worked to increase tourism in the Yucatan.

In 2010, the Mexican state of Yucatan purchased most of the land at the site of Chichen Itza from the Barbachano family, except for the Hacienda Chichen. The hotel continues to host tourists who are eager to stay so close to the famous ruins.

# CHAPTER 10
## A Living Culture

Today, there are over six million Maya still living in the region. They are spread throughout Guatemala, Belize, Honduras, El Salvador, and four Mexican states. They speak over thirty dialects of the Mayan language. They honor the traditions of their ancestors, including a deep respect for their cenotes. Maya women are known for their woven cloth and beautiful embroidery. There are Maya priests, still called shamans, who continue to keep the 260-day Round Count calendar. The modern shamans give spiritual advice and lead religious rituals, just as the ancient priests did.

The Classic Maya were known for their artistry, writing, math, astronomy, and political

Maya women in Belize

complexity. Chichen Itza is proof of their great achievements. Its buildings stand today as an example of the Maya mastery of trade, commerce, language, and art.

In 2007, Chichen Itza was classified as one the New Seven Wonders of the World, along with the Taj Mahal, the Roman Colosseum, and the sites of Machu Picchu and Petra. It was also named a UNESCO World Heritage Site in 1988.

Chichen Itza is one of the most popular tourist destinations in the world. Between 3,500 and 5,000 people visit *each day*! They are asked to be respectful of the ancient buildings, which become more fragile every year. Starting in 2006, tourists were no longer allowed to climb

El Castillo. But, over a thousand years after it was built, the mighty pyramid at Chichen Itza continues to amaze the people who come to see it.

# World Heritage Sites

The United Nations Educational, Scientific, and Cultural Organization (UNESCO) chooses sites or landmarks that have a cultural, historical, or scientific importance and provides legal protection for them.

Most of these sites are geographically or historically unique. Sometimes they represent an amazing accomplishment, like the Taos Pueblo and the Great Wall of China. Other World Heritage sites, like the Great Barrier Reef, and Yellowstone and Everglades National Parks, are natural wonders. Millions of people visit World Heritage sites every year.

As of 2019, there are 1,121 World Heritage sites in more than 160 countries.

Yellowstone National Park

During the spring equinox, around March 21, and the fall equinox, around September 23, visitors assemble in the large plaza surrounding El Castillo. They come to watch the majestic return of Kukulkan, just as the Maya did for hundreds of years. They gather to see the shadowy illusion of the serpent god along the side of the great pyramid. Although this magical scene lasts only a few hours each year, it is a huge event that draws people from all over the world.

To understand how remarkable this truly is, we must remember that the Maya built this massive pyramid according to an exact plan. They knew where each stone had to be positioned in order to create this spectacular effect. Their impressive engineering at Chichen Itza demonstrates not only their superb mathematical skills but also their deep understanding of the natural world around them, and their respect for the life-giving forces of nature.

It is an awe-inspiring achievement.

# Timeline of Chichen Itza

| | |
|---|---|
| 250–900 | The Classic Period of the ancient Maya civilization |
| 415–455 | A settlement at Chichen Itza is founded |
| c. 600 | Major building projects are begun at Chichen Itza |
| c. 800–900 | El Castillo is built at Chichen Itza |
| c. 900 | Chichen Itza reaches its peak as the Maya center of power and trade |
| 1220 | A new Maya capital is established at Mayapan |
| 1450 | Mayapan loses power, and the Maya begin to scatter to smaller villages and towns |
| 1533 | The Spanish conquistadors fail in their attempt to make Chichen Itza their capital city |
| 1697 | The last ancient Maya city is captured and destroyed by the Spanish |
| 1841 | John Lloyd Stephens and Frederick Catherwood travel to Central America and document the ruins of Chichen Itza |
| 1988 | Chichen Itza is named a UNESCO World Heritage site |
| 2007 | Chichen Itza is classified as one of the New Seven Wonders of the World |
| 2010 | The Mexican state of Yucatan purchases most of the land at the Chichen Itza site from the Barbachano family |

# Timeline of the World

324 — Constantine becomes the undisputed Roman emperor and founds Rome's new capital at Constantinople

795 — Vikings first raid Ireland

1096 — European crusaders begin to assemble at Constantinople during the First Crusade

c. 1280 — The Maori colonize New Zealand

1487 — The great pyramid at Tenochtitlan (inside present-day Mexico City) is inaugurated by the Aztecs

1727 — The Portuguese bring the coffee plant to Brazil

1773 — British colonists in North America dump tea into Boston Harbor in protest of the Tea Act and British taxation

1863 — The Battle of Gettysburg, the largest battle of the American Civil War, is fought in southern Pennsylvania from July 1 to 3

1889 — American journalist Nellie Bly begins her journey, traveling around the world in less than eighty days

1930 — American astronomer Clyde Tombaugh discovers Pluto

2012 — Activist Malala Yousafzai recovers from being shot by a Taliban gunman in Pakistan

# Bibliography

**\*Books for young readers**

Carlsen, William. *Jungle of Stone: The True Story of Two Men, Their Extraordinary Journey, and the Discovery of the Lost Civilization of the Maya.* New York: William Morrow, 2016.

\*Clynes, Tom. "The Mysteries of the Maya Revealed." *New York Times for Kids*, April 28, 2019.

DK. *Timelines of History*. New York: Dorling Kindersley, 2011.

Harasta, Jesse, and Charles River Editors. *Chichen Itza: The History and Mystery of the Maya's Most Famous City*. Ann Arbor: Charles River Editors, 2013.

\*Honders, Christine. *Ancient Maya Culture*. New York: Rosen Publishing Group, 2017.

\*Kule, Elaine. *Amazing Ancients! World of the Maya*. New York: Penguin Workshop, 2019.

\*Kule, Elaine. *Exploring the Ancient Maya*. Mankato, MN: 12-Story Library, 2018.

Landa, Friar Diego de. *Yucatan Before and After the Conquest*, translated with notes by William Gates. New York: Dover Publications, 1978.

\*Maloy, Jackie. *The Ancient Maya*. New York: Children's Press, 2010.

"Maya Apocalypse Mysteries." **Unearthed**. Composed of episodes
"Mayan City of Blood" (season 1, episode 1) and "Lost City of
the Maya" (season 4, episode 9). Aired January 5, 2019, on the
Science Channel.

O'Neill, Zora, and Fisher, John. **The Rough Guide to the Yucatán**.
New York: Rough Guides, 2008.